How Smart is Your Pet?

Take a good look at your dog or cat. On a scale of 1 to 10, just how smart do you think he or she is?

Think of all the smart things your pet does. Does your dog sit on command? Does your cat have several ways of telling you what she wants? Does your dog stare at you when he's hungry? Does your cat go to the door when she wants out?

Overall, how would you rate your pet's intelligence? Is your pet...

❏ a canine/feline Einstein?

❏ as dumb as a doornail?

❏ just about average?

The tests in this book are a fun way to *estimate* how smart your pet is. Unfortunately, they can't speak (or meow) for the most important thing—how much you love your pet, and how much he or she loves you!

Tips on How to Test Your Pet

Your *How Smart is Your Pet?* kit comes with a flying disc, two "find the hidden treat" cups, a squeaker, and two terrific Certificates of Achievement.

In addition, you'll need to gather a few things from around the house for some of the tests:

- *dry* pet food treats that don't smell too much
- a large towel
- aluminum foil
- yarn or string
- a large paper grocery bag
- a stopwatch (or a wristwatch or clock with a second hand)

> **CAUTION**
>
> ## While conducting these tests
>
> ★ Never bother your pet while he or she is eating.
>
> ★ Never tease your pet.
>
> ★ Don't put your face in front of your dog or cat's face. (Your pet may have test anxiety, too!)
>
> ★ Check around after you've tested your pet. (You don't want a treat to rot anywhere!)
>
> ★ Don't let your pet chew on the disc, cups, or squeaker in this kit—they're for testing, not eating!

All About Dog Intelligence

Dogs and humans have been companions for over six thousand years. During this time, dogs have proven their intelligence and loyalty in many ways.

At first, dogs were used as herders, hunters, and watchdogs. In exchange, they received food and shelter. Later, they served as guides and even transportation, like sled dogs.

More recently, dogs have been trained as companions for people who are physically challenged, as athletes, and even as actors.

Dogs inherited their well-developed brain and their top-notch hearing and smelling abilities from their ancestor, the wolf.

Although your dog may not be a trained superstar, he or she probably has managed to find a way into your heart and home (and maybe even your bed!).

Your dog eats, sleeps, and plays all day—and doesn't have to do *any* chores or homework. Now who's the smart one?

What's Your Pet's Name?
We've used all different dog and cat names throughout this book. We hope we've used your pet's name!

Smartest & Most Obedient Breeds

1. Border Collie
2. Poodle
3. German Shepherd
4. Golden Retriever
5. Doberman Pinscher
6. Shetland Sheepdog
7. Labrador Retriever
8. Papillion
9. Rottweiler
10. Australian Cattle Dog

Source: American and Canadian Kennel Clubs

Doggie Detective Tests

Dog Test #1 *(Problem Solving)*

Materials: one cup, dog treat, stopwatch
Directions: Show Mona a food treat. Let her get a good sniff. Put the treat on the floor. Cover it with the cup. Start the stopwatch.

Check One

5 pts ____She finds the treat within 15 seconds.
4 pts ____...within 15 to 30 seconds.
3 pts ____...within 30 to 60 seconds.
2 pts ____She sniffs, but doesn't find the treat.
1 pt <None>She doesn't even try to find the treat.

Make sure your dog doesn't try to eat the cup!

Dog Test #2 *(Short Term Memory)*

Materials: two cups, dog treat, stopwatch
Directions: Lightly rub the treat on the inside of both cups so they smell the same. Place them about one foot apart on the floor. While Lucky is watching, place the treat under one of the cups. Slowly move the cups around to try to confuse him. Hold him back for 10 seconds, then start the stopwatch.

Check One

5 pts ____He finds the treat within 15 seconds.
4 pts ____...within 15 to 30 seconds.
3 pts ____...within 30 to 60 seconds.
2 pts ____He sniffs, but doesn't find the treat.
1 pt ____He doesn't even try to find the treat.

The Undercover Test

Dog Test #3 *(Problem Solving)*

Materials: large towel, stopwatch
Directions: With one quick move, cover Maggie's head and front shoulders with the towel. Start the stopwatch. See how long it takes her to free herself completely.

Check One

- 5 pts ____ 15 seconds
- 4 pts ____ 15 to 30 seconds
- 3 pts ____ 30 to 60 seconds
- 2 pts ____ 1 to 2 minutes
- 1 pt ____ Maggie just sits there. (Check to see if she's asleep—or at least breathing!)

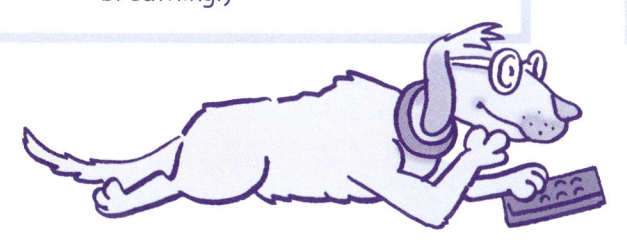

The TV Test

Dog Test #4 *(Visual and Audio skills)*

Materials: TV set
Directions: When a TV program or commercial comes on featuring a barking dog, watch what Buddy does.

Check One

- 5 pts ____ He sees the dog and gets excited or barks.
- 4 pts ____ He sees the dog and whines in confusion.
- 3 pts ____ He watches intently, but doesn't "get" that dogs are on TV.
- 2 pts ____ He looks in the direction of the screen.
- 1 pt ____ He ignores the TV or falls asleep.

The Fetch Test

Dog Test #5 *(Coordination & Retrieval)*

Materials: flying disc
Directions: Toss the disc away from you—nice and easy so that Max can chase and try to catch it.

Check One

- 5 pts ____ He catches it and returns it.
- 4 pts ____ He misses it, goes after it, and returns it.
- 3 pts ____ He goes after it and plays "keep-away."
- 2 pts ____ He grabs it, lies down, and tries to chew it.
- 1 pt ____ He walks away and does something else.

Don't let Max chew or eat the disc! Bring it out only for tossing and retrieval.

The Treat in the Corner Test

Dog Test #6 *(Short-Term Memory)*

Materials: dog treat, stopwatch
Directions: Have Molly sit and stay in the center of a room. Show her the treat. Place the treat on the floor in a corner while she watches. Lead her out of the room for *15 seconds* and return. Let her loose. Start the stopwatch.

Check One

- 5 pts ____ She goes straight for the food.
- 4 pts ____ She sniffs around very carefully and goes straight to it.
- 3 pts ____ She sniffs around randomly and finds it within 45 seconds.
- 2 pts ____ She sniffs around but doesn't find it within 45 seconds.
- 1 pt ____ She makes no effort to find the treat.

The Treat in the Other Corner Test

Dog Test #7 *(Long-Term Memory)*

Materials: dog treat, stopwatch
Directions: Give this test right after Test #6. Do the same set up. Make sure Molly sees you place the treat in a *different* corner than before. Lead her out of the room for *five minutes* and return. Let her loose. Start the stopwatch.

Check One

- 5 pts ____ She goes straight for the food.
- 4 pts ____ She goes to the corner where the treat from test #6 was, then quickly goes to the correct corner.
- 3 pts ____ She sniffs along the edges of the room and finds it.
- 2 pts ____ She sniffs around randomly and finds it within 45 seconds.
- 1 pt ____ What treat?

The Squeaker Test

Dog Test #8 *(Trainability)*

Materials: squeaker, dog treat
Directions: Find a trick Cocoa hasn't mastered, such as "roll over." After you tell (and help) her roll over, immediately squeak the squeaker, give her a treat, and praise her. When Cocoa has mastered the task, eliminate the food. Eventually, you can eliminate the squeaker, too. *Note: Limit training to about 10 minutes a day.*

After about 4 days of training, check one

- 5 pts ____ She rolls over when you give a verbal command.
- 4 pts ____ ...when you give a verbal command and hand signal
- 3 pts ____ ...when she sees the food treat.
- 2 pts ____ She lies on her back waiting for a belly rub.
- 1 pt ____ She just looks up at you and wags her tail.

The Couch Potato Test

Dog Test #9 *(Problem Solving)*

Materials: a couch that your dog can reach under, but can't put his head under; dog treat; stopwatch
Directions: After Harry sniffs the treat, place it (within reach) under the couch.

Check One

- 5 pts ____ He uses a paw to get the treat in 60 seconds.
- 4 pts ____ He uses a paw to get the treat within 3 minutes.
- 3 pts ____ He uses his nose only and doesn't get the treat in three minutes.
- 2 pts ____ He sniffs and gives up.
- 1 pt ____ He doesn't try to get the treat.

The Tree Tangle Test

Dog Test #10 *(Problem Solving)*

Materials: dog leash, sturdy tree, stopwatch
Directions: Take Ruby outside on her leash. (Tell an adult what you are doing.) Wrap the leash around a tree or pole once. Can Ruby untangle herself? Call her name and see what she does.

Check One

- 5 pts: ____ She untangles the leash within 30 seconds.
- 4 pts: ____ ...within 60 seconds.
- 3 pts: ____ She gets tangled up worse!
- 2 pts: ____ She digs a hole.
- 1 pt: ____ She lies down.

All About Cat Intelligence

Because cats are independent hunters, they don't run in packs and they don't look to humans as their leaders. But cats understand that if they want to eat and be loved, they have to abide by at least some rules!

If one definition of intelligence is "the ability to learn," then cats are very intelligent.

Does your cat come running when he hears the can opener or the rattle of a food dish? Does he know when you're leaving for school? Has he learned to use a scratching post instead of the sofa?

Actually, most cats are so smart they have their owners trained. You buy your cat the best cat food, feed him when he's good and ready, and let him sleep wherever he wants to sleep!

Cats get away with crazy behavior because we think they aren't smart enough to know better. But, hey—your cat eats, sleeps, and plays *all* day. Who's the smart one?

The Jungle Hunter Test

Cat Test #1 *(Ability to Pay Attention)*

Materials: foil "mouse," stopwatch (To make the mouse, wad a piece of foil into a ball. Tie pieces of yarn or string around it so the mouse has lots of tails.)

Directions: Move the foil mouse around on the floor with your hand to get Missy's attention. Start the stopwatch.

Check One

- 5 pts _____ She plays with it for at least 60 seconds.
- 4 pts _____ ...for up to 30 seconds.
- 3 pts _____ ...for about 10 seconds.
- 2 pts _____ She sniffs but doesn't bother to play with it.
- 1 pt _____ She walks away with her tail in the air.

The Mouse Trap Test

Cat Test #2 *(Problem Solving)*

Materials: disc, foil "mouse," stopwatch

Directions: Get Milo interested in your foil mouse. Put the mouse on the ground and cover it with the disc. Start the stopwatch.

Check One

- 5 pts _____ He uncovers the mouse within 5 seconds.
- 4 pts _____ ...within 5 to 15 seconds.
- 3 pts _____ ...within 15 to 60 seconds.
- 2 pts _____ He sniffs but doesn't get the mouse.
- 1 pts _____ He ignores you or makes no effort to get the mouse.

Roll 'Em Test

Cat Test #3 *(Visual Skills)*

Materials: one cup, stopwatch
Directions: Roll the cup past Nutmeg.

Check One

- 5 pts ____ She runs and grabs it within 5 seconds.
- 4 pts ____ She watches, waits for it to stop, then darts for it.
- 3 pts ____ She walks up to it and pokes it curiously.
- 2 pt ____ She looks at you in disgust.
- 1 pt ____ She's too busy to bother and leaves the room.

The Bow Test

Cat Test #4 *(Problem Solving)*

Materials: A scarf or bandana, stopwatch
Directions: Loosely tie a bow around Lou-Lou's tail or front paw.

Check One

- 5 pts ____ She unties the bow within 30 seconds.
- 4 pts ____ ...within 2 minutes.
- 3 pts ____ She wiggles the bow off of her tail or paw within 30 seconds.
- 2 pts ____ ... within 2 minutes.
- 1 pt ____ She looks cute wearing a bow. It's her color.

The Food-Line Test

Cat Test #5 *(Paying Attention)*

Materials: five cat treats, stopwatch
Directions: Put out a line of five treats spaced about two feet apart. See if Angel investigates the whole trail. (It doesn't matter if she eats or just sniffs them. She's not a dog!)

Check One

- 5 pts _____ She follows the whole trail and eats or sniffs each treat.
- 4 pts _____ She sniffs two or three treats and walks away.
- 3 pts _____ She bats the treats around like a toy.
- 2 pts _____ She ignores the treats and stares at you—wondering what you're up to.
- 1 pt _____ She ignores the treats completely and walks away.

The "Come and Get It" Test

Cat Test #6 *(Audio & Memory Skills)*

Materials: your cat's "dinner bell" cues
Directions: What says "time to eat" for Sylvester? The can opener? Shaking a bag of dry cat food? Banging the dish on the counter? Sound Sylvester's "dinner bell" at an *unusual* time of the day or in a *different* place than normal.

Check One

- 5 pts _____ He comes running.
- 4 pts _____ He eventually walks over to check it out.
- 3 pts _____ He perks up, checks the clock, and goes back to sleep.
- 2 pts _____ He raises a whisker, but doesn't move.
- 1 pts _____ He doesn't get the connection between the sound and meal time.

The "A Cat by Any Other Name" Test

Cat Test #7 *(Audio & Memory Skills)*

Materials: your voice
Directions: Call Sassy using another name, but use the same tone of voice as your usual call.

Check One

- 5 pts ____ She looks at you as if to say, "You don't mean me, do you?"
- 4 pts ____ She recognizes the tone, but doesn't respond to the wrong name.
- 3 pts ____ She doesn't respond at all.
- 2 pts ____ She comes as if her name had been called.
- 1 pt ____ She comes, although she hardly ever comes when called.

"Give a dog food and you're a hero. Give a cat food and she acts as if you're making an offering to Her Highness." —*Unknown*

The "Don't Let the Cat Out of the Bag" Test

Cat Test #8 *(Problem Solving)*

Materials: large paper grocery bag, stopwatch
Directions: Set the bag on the floor and guide Toby into the bag.

Check One

- 5 pts ____ He escapes within 10 seconds and walks away in disgust.
- 4 pts ____ He starts playing in it. (After all, he is a cat!)
- 3 pts ____ He escapes within 10 to 30 seconds.
- 2 pts ____ He escapes within 30 to 60 seconds.
- 1 pts ____ He just sits inside the bag.

The Stool Fool Test

Cat Test #9 *(Problem Solving)*

Materials: stool, table, cat treat, stopwatch
Directions: Set a stool near a high table. Place the cat treat on the table. See if Princess can figure out how to get it.

Check One

- 5 pts ____ She climbs up and gets the treat within 10 seconds.
- 4 pts ____ She gets the treat within 10 to 20 seconds.
- 3 pts ____ She gets the treat within 20 to 60 seconds.
- 2 pts ____ She sniffs the air but doesn't get the treat.
- 1 pt ____ She makes no effort to get the treat.

The Pillow Puss Test

Cat Test #10 *(Trainability)*

Materials: A pillow on the floor, squeaker
Directions: Call Boots. Pat the pillow and say, "Boots. On the pillow." When she touches the pillow, immediately squeak the squeaker, give her a treat, and praise her. When Boots has mastered the task, eliminate the food. Eventually, you can eliminate the squeaker, too. *Note: Limit training to about 10 minutes a day.*

After about 6 days of training, check one:

- 5 pts ____ She leaps on the pillow like a proud puss.
- 4 pts ____ She sits on the pillow after you show her a treat.
- 3 pts ____ She heads your way and walks away.
- 2 pts ____ She looks at you as if to say, "You don't mean me do you?"
- 1 pt ____ She ignores you completely.

Sensational Scoring

Your pet could score from 1 to 5 points on each test. Note that he or she could get 1 point just for showing up!

The maximum score is 50 points (10 tests times 5 points each—you do the math!). While this scoring system is not exactly scientific, we've come up with these special dog- and cat-agories:

Total Points	Award
40 to 50 ⇨	Canine/Feline Einstein
30 to 39 ⇨	Extremely Intelligent (or an extremely good faker)
20 to 29 ⇨	Brighter than the Average Stone
10 to 19 ⇨	Blissfully Ignorant (but totally lovable!)
0 to 9 ⇨	Dumb as a Doornail (or far too smart to bother with your silly "intelligence" test!)

Certificate of Achievement

Whether your pet is a genius—or ingenious enough to get out of taking intelligence tests—he or she deserves a Certificate of Achievement!

Complete your pet's certificate, draw your pet's picture or attach a photo, and display it in a special place.

If you administer the tests again, feel free to change the score.

And, don't forget to give your best friend a big hug for being the most lovable pet in the world.

Things We Can Learn from Our Dog...

- ★ When someone you love comes home, run to greet them.
- ★ Whenever you're happy, dance around and wag your entire body.
- ★ Never bite when a simple growl will do.
- ★ If what you want lies buried, dig until you find it.
- ★ Be loyal and kind.

Things We Can Learn from Our Cat...

- ★ Never pretend to be something you're not.
- ★ Let others know when they've invaded your territory.
- ★ Take lots of naps.
- ★ When in doubt, wash your face.
- ★ Be proud of who you are.
- ★ Remember that attitude is *everything!*